THE CANADIAN BRASS

BOOK OF INTERMEDIATE TRUMPET SOLOS

Edited by **Fred Mills** and **Ron Romm**
of The Canadian Brass

■

All Selections Performed by
Fred Mills and **Ron Romm** on trumpet,
and pianist Bill Casey

■

Plus Piano Accompaniments Only

The instrument pictured on the cover is a CB10 Trumpet from The Canadian Brass Collection,
a line of professional brass instruments marketed by The Canadian Brass.

Photo: Gordon Janowiak

Speed • Pitch • Balance • Loop

To access audio visit:
www.halleonard.com/mylibrary
Enter Code
6658-8614-1475-4476

ISBN 978-0-7935-7253-3

7777 W. BLUEMOUND RD. P.O. BOX 13819 MILWAUKEE, WI 53213

www.canadianbrass.com
www.halleonard.com

CONTENTS

In progressive order of difficulty, from a generally intermediate to a more advanced level.

* recorded by Fred Mills, trumpet
** recorded by Ron Romm, trumpet

To All Fellow Brass Players:

Those of us who teach and play brass instruments know what a struggle it can be to find interesting and beautiful solos for our instruments. We ourselves experienced the problem first hand in our younger days, and later have encountered the same shortage of solo material at various points in our lives when we have taught brass students. It's been an aim of ours to add to the solo repertory, and we are particularly pleased to add these collections to our library of Canadian Brass publications.

What makes a good brass solo? There is virtually no original literature for our instruments, beyond a handful of trumpet and horn concertos, before the twentieth century. So if, as brass players, we want to play Bach or Handel or Mozart or Brahms, then we must choose pieces written for other instruments to transcribe for our own. And how do we choose what to transcribe? In our opinion, vocal music offers the best solution for various reasons. The pieces are often short, which is best for a brass solo. The music is written originally to words, which makes each piece have a strong emotional content and point of view that can be very satisfying to play. Because in the broadest definition the voice could be defined as a wind instrument, the phrases and lines are naturally well suited for brass players. And further, there is simply far more solo music written for the voice than any other instrument in history. Composers seem to have been continually inspired by singers throughout the centuries, and we see no reason why we brass players shouldn't benefit from all that inspiration! After having said all of that, it will come as no surprise to state that most of the pieces we have chosen for these solo books are transcriptions of vocal pieces. Another priority in making the selections was to include mostly work by major composers from the history of music. Altogether too much of the educational solo music available almost exclusively presents work by minor or unknown composers.

The recordings we have made should be used only as a guide for you to use in studying a piece. We certainly didn't go into these recording sessions with the idea of trying to create any kind of "definitive performances" of this music. There is no such thing as a definitive performance anyway. Each musician, being a unique individual, will naturally always come up with a slightly different rendition of a piece of music. We often find that students are timid about revealing their own ideas and personalities when going beyond the notes on the page in making music. After you've practiced for weeks or months on a piece of music, and have mastered all the technical requirements, you certainly have earned the right to play it in the way you think it sounds best! It may not be the way your friend would play it, or the way The Canadian Brass would play it. But you will have made the music your own, and that's what counts.

Good luck and Happy Brass Playing!
The Canadian Brass

FRED MILLS had an extensive performing career that preceded his joining The Canadian Brass. He grew up in Guelph, Ontario. After graduating from the Juilliard School of Music, he became principal trumpet under conductor Leopold Stokowski in both the American and Houston Symphonies. He also performed under Pablo Casals at the Casals Festival, and has played at the Marlboro Music Festival. For six years Fred was principal trumpet of the New York City Opera orchestra. Following this, he returned to Canada to take a position as principal trumpet of the then newly formed National Arts Centre Orchestra in Ottawa. In 1996, after 23 years with the ensemble, Fred chose to come off the road and lend his expertise to students at the University of Georgia.

ABOUT THE MUSIC...

George Philipp Telemann: Trumpet Air

Bach's German contemporary, George Philipp Telemann (1681-1767) was extremely prolific, and during his lifetime he was considered to be Germany's greatest composer. (Bach was not widely known or esteemed as a composer during his lifetime.) Telemann is credited with being the first composer to present a modern style public concert, with various works on the same program. (Pronunciation tip: Telemann=TELL-eh-mahn)

Gabriel Fauré: Lydia

Fauré (1845-1924) was one of France's major nineteenth century composers, turning out operas, piano music, orchestra music, chamber works, and choral pieces (the Requiem is well known). But more than any other composer in French history, Fauré excelled in setting poetry to music for the voice to sing, and his many, many songs are at the center of the international repertory of art songs. Fauré became the most important music professor in France, revered for decades at the Paris Conservatoire as the teacher of every French musician of worth. (Pronunciation tip: Fauré=four-AY)

Henry Purcell: Rondeau

For some reason, difficult to explain, in the 18th and 19th centuries there were virtually no British composers of the stature of the major composers on the European continent. Prior to the 20th century, the last world class composer from England was Henry Purcell (1659-1695). He grew up in a prominent musical family and had the training that allowed him contact with the elite musical circles. He became organist of Westminster Abbey at the age of 20, and remained in royal appointments for the rest of his short life. He composed extensively for the theatre, providing incidental music for plays and also operas. He is buried in Westminster Abbey. (Pronunciation tips: Purcell=PUR-sul, *not* accented on the second syllable, as in pur-SEL; Rondeau= Ron-doe).

Alessandro Scarlatti: Arietta (Gia il sole dal Gange)

Alessandro Scarlatti (1660-1725) was a leading Italian composer of his time, especially noted for his operas and cantatas. (Most Italian music of the time was written for voice.) Born in Sicily, little is known about his early life except that at some point he moved to Rome before his twentieth year, and had some musical training in that city. Respected and admired as a composer by several important patrons in European royalty, he settled in Naples in the 1680s, and was the most powerful musical figure in the region for over two decades. "Arietta" is from one of his many operas, none of which are still performed.

Giuseppe Verdi: Gypsy Song from *Il Trovatore*

Giuseppe Verdi (1813-1901) was the most profound, prolific and revered composer of Italian opera in the 19th century. *Il Trovatore* (The Troubadour) is one of his masterworks, and was premiered in 1853.   In the plot, a band of gypsies has been singing as they labor at their anvils by the fire ("The Anvil Chorus"). Then the old woman, Azucena, vividly tells the tale of how her mother was burned at the stake in this haunting gypsy song. (Pronunciation tips: Verdi=VAIR-dee, Trovatore=tro-vah-TOR-ay)

Gilbert and Sullivan: Dance a Cachucha from *The Gondoliers*

The great English operetta creators, Gilbert and Sullivan, were the Rodgers and Hammerstein of their day, creating the equivalent of Broadway musical comedies for London of the 1880s and 1890s. Arthur Sullivan wrote the music and W. S. Gilbert wrote the witty and politically satirical words. Their shows, such as *H.M.S. Pinafore, The Mikado,* and *Pirates of Penzance*, are still very popular. It's interesting that though celebrated and successful in their collaboration, Sullivan and Gilbert never particularly liked one another, and had public battles on more than one occasion. (Pronunciation tip: Cachucha=ka-CHOO-cha)

Johannes Brahms: Serenade (Ständchen)

The great German romantic master Johannes Brahms (1833-1897) spent his life composing every type of piece (except opera), including symphonies, concertos, chamber music, piano music, organ music, and choral music. Like most other composers of the 19th century he composed a great number of songs for voice and piano, and Brahms was certainly a master of the genre.

Franz Schubert: The Brook (Wohin?)

Schubert (pronounced SHU-bayrt) (1797-1828) was the first master of German song literature, or *lieder,* composing over 600 songs for voice and piano during his lifetime. "The Brook" (the original German title is "Wohin?"— literally meaning "Wither?") is from the great song cycle "Die Schöne Müllerin" (The Beautiful Maid of the Mill), a collection of twenty songs that, in the sequence of the poetry, tells a story of a miller, his search for love and his betrayal. "The Brook" comes early in the story, and is a song about wondering where a brooklet might lead. You can actually hear the effect of the rippling water of the flowing brook in the piano part.

Scott Joplin: Solace

Scott Joplin (1868-1917) is universally recognized as the most accomplished master of the Ragtime style. Considering this, it's difficult to believe that for most of this century his music languished in obscurity. Joplin's piano pieces were popular during his lifetime, but soon after his death in 1917 his music fell out of the repertory. One can't help but believe that if he had lived just a decade longer, more into the mature recording age, that itwould have been a different story. But works of high caliber usually do not go unnoticed forever. The Joplin revival began in the 1970s, and since that time (particularly after the hit movie "The Sting") his music has been played and loved all over the world. "Solace," written in 1909, is one of Joplin's most elegant rags for piano.

Claude Debussy: Mandolin

Arguably the most important French composer who ever lived, Claude Debussy (1812-1918) wrote music that is often labeled as "impressionism," a musical counterpart to the French painting style of the late nineteenth century. He wrote operas, ballets, orchestral pieces, chamber music, piano music, and vocal music. "Mandolin" is one of his more than eighty songs for voice and piano. The poem is about men serenading with their mandolins a group of ladies on a beautiful warm evening in the moonlight.

George Frideric Handel: Cleopatra's Lament (Piangero, la sorte mia)
from *Julius Caesar*

Handel (1685-1759) was one of the two musical giants of the Baroque (the other being J. S. Bach, of course). Handel spent most of his life in London, running an opera company, and writing 45 operas in 30 years. When he started losing money on opera in London, he switched to composing oratorio with equal fury, and kept his fame and fortune afloat. This famous lament is in a *da capo* form, meaning a first section of music, a new section of middle music, and then a repeat of the first section once more, usually with ornamentation. As Cleopatra ponders her suicide she sings this profoundly beautiful music. We have provided written out ornamentation for the *da capo*, but feel free to change this as it suits you.

Giachino Rossini: La Danza (The Dance)

Rossini (1792-1868) was one of the more colorful eccentrics in music history. Enormous success came to him as an opera composer at a very young age. He had his first commission for an opera at the age of 18, and by the age of 24 he had written what would be his most famous music, *The Barber of Seville.* (When you live to be 76, it's pretty tough have the biggest success of your life at age 24.) He composed operas for twenty years, sometimes usually going from city to city to write his commissions, composing the opera in a matter of a few weeks, supervising the premiere, and then moving on to the next city. His final opera was William Tell in 1829, from which the famous "Lone Ranger" overture is taken. He retired in Paris at the age of 37, and remained there a man of leisure for nearly forty years. "La Danza" is one of the pieces written during the Paris years of retirement, and is a familiar tune around the world. It's probably best known in our time as a favorite encore of Luciano Pavarotti. (Pronunciation tip: Danza=DAHN-zah)

TRUMPET AIR

George Phillipp Telemann

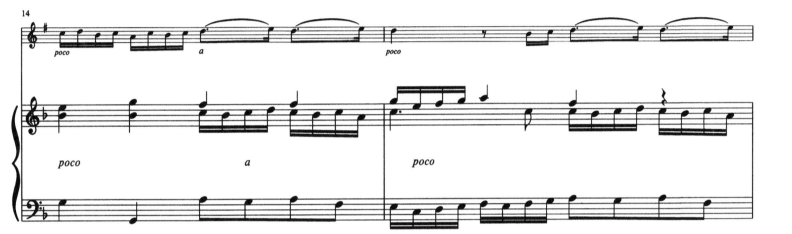

LYDIA

Gabriel Faure

RONDEAU

Henry Purcell

ARIETTA
(Gia il sole dal Gange)

Alessandro Scarlatti

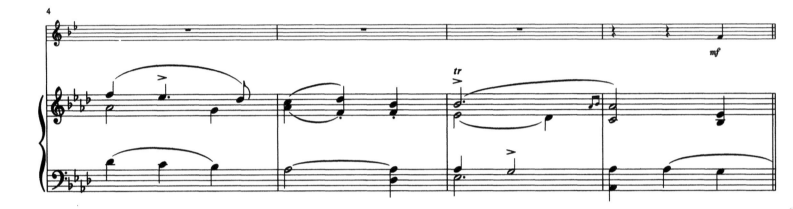

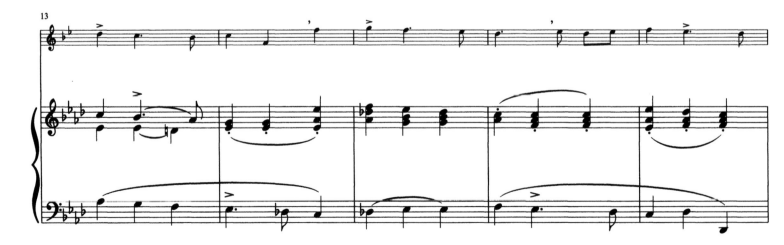

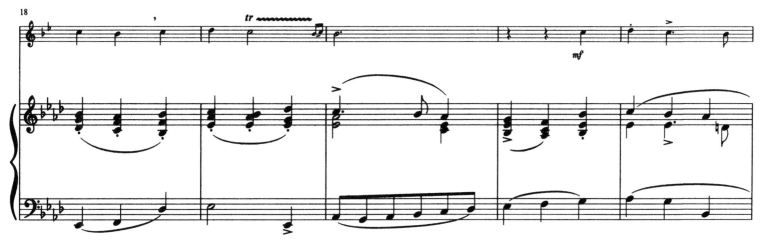

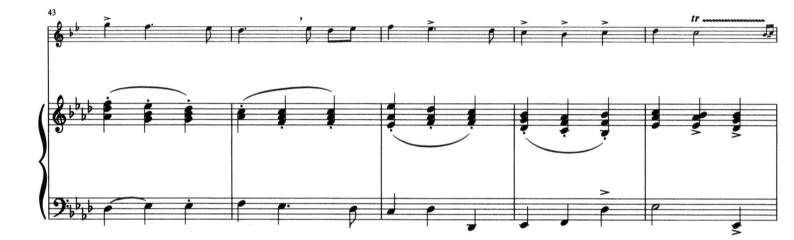

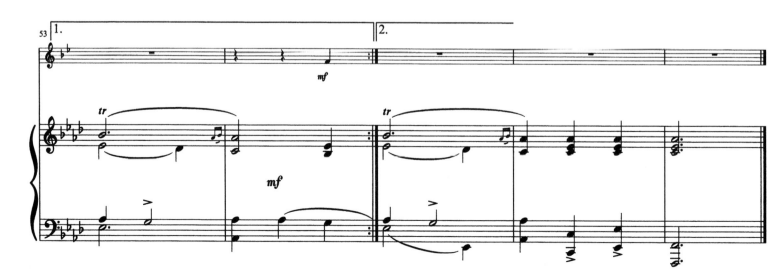

GYPSY SONG

(Stride la vampa!)

from
IL TROVATORE

Giuseppe Verdi

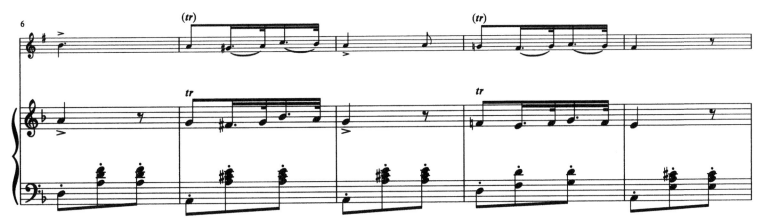

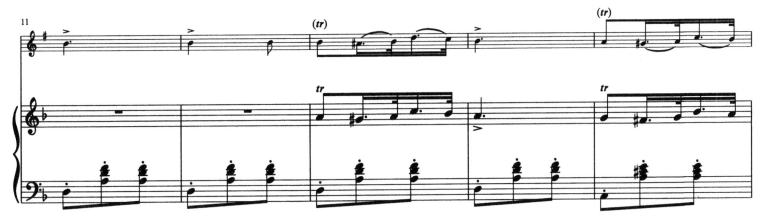

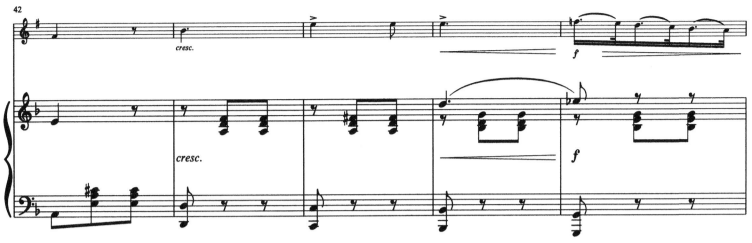

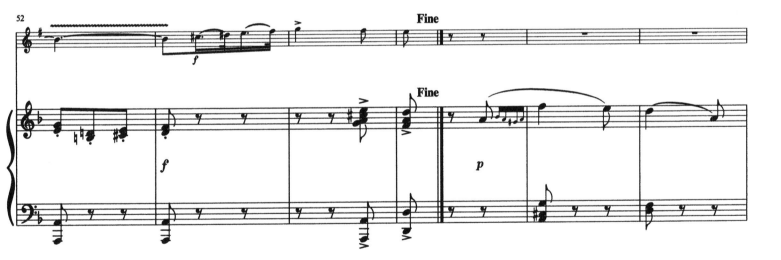

DANCE A CACHUCHA

from
THE GONDOLIERS

words by W.S. Gilbert
music by Arthur Sullivan

SERENADE
(Ständchen)

Johannes Brahms

THE BROOK
(Wohin?)

Franz Schubert

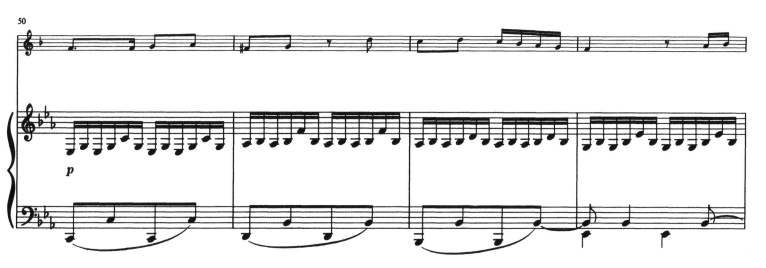

SOLACE

Scott Joplin
arr. by Rick Walters

Repeats are optional throughout.

MANDOLIN

Claude Debussy

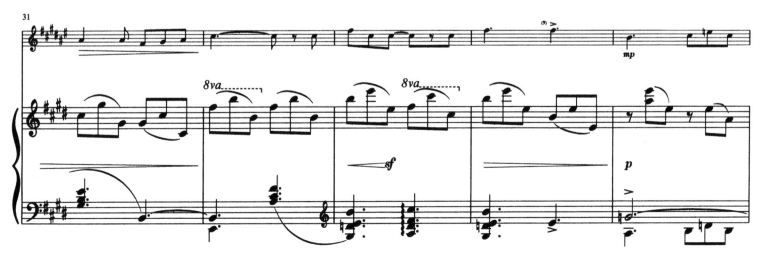

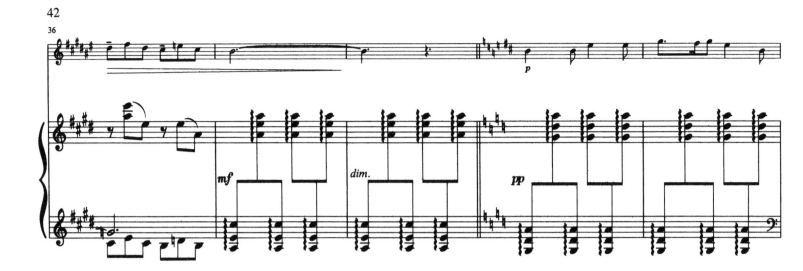

CLEOPATRA'S LAMENT
(Piangero, la sorte mia)
from
JULIUS CAESAR

George Frideric Handel

Largo
First Time

Trumpet

Da Capo

Piano

LA DANZA
(The Dance)
Neopolitan Tarantella

Gioachino Rossini

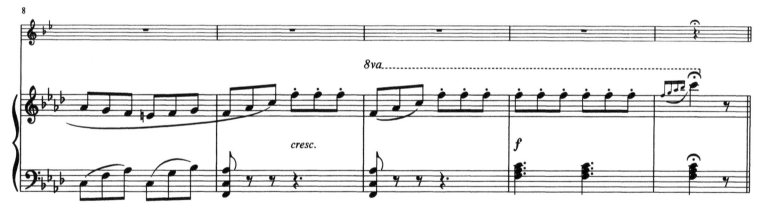

2nd time only

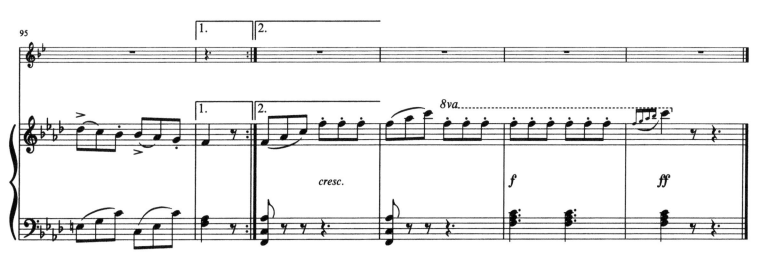

THE CANADIAN BRASS

BOOK OF INTERMEDIATE TRUMPET SOLOS

Edited by **Fred Mills** and **Ron Romm**
of The Canadian Brass

■

All Selections Performed by
Fred Mills and **Ron Romm, trumpets,**
and Bill Casey, Piano

■

Plus Piano Accompaniments Only

CONTENTS

In progressive order of difficulty, from a generally intermediate to a more advanced level.

ISBN 978-0-7935-7253-3

HAL•LEONARD®
7777 W. BLUEMOUND RD. P.O. BOX 13819 MILWAUKEE, WI 53213

www.canadianbrass.com
www.halleonard.com

To All Fellow Brass Players:

Those of us who teach and play brass instruments know what a struggle it can be to find interesting and beautiful solos for our instruments. We ourselves experienced the problem first hand in our younger days, and later have encountered the same shortage of solo material at various points in our lives when we have taught brass students. It's been an aim of ours to add to the solo repertory, and we are particularly pleased to add these collections to our library of Canadian Brass publications.

What makes a good brass solo? There is virtually no original literature for our instruments, beyond a handful of trumpet and horn concertos, before the twentieth century. So if, as brass players, we want to play Bach or Handel or Mozart or Brahms, then we must choose pieces written for other instruments to transcribe for our own. And how do we choose what to transcribe? In our opinion, vocal music offers the best solution for various reasons. The pieces are often short, which is best for a brass solo. The music is written originally to words, which makes each piece have a strong emotional content and point of view that can be very satisfying to play. Because in the broadest definition the voice could be defined as a wind instrument, the phrases and lines are naturally well suited for brass players. And further, there is simply far more solo music written for the voice than any other instrument in history. Composers seem to have been continually inspired by singers throughout the centuries, and we see no reason why we brass players shouldn't benefit from all that inspiration! After having said all of that, it will come as no surprise to state that most of the pieces we have chosen for these solo books are transcriptions of vocal pieces. Another priority in making the selections was to include mostly work by major composers from the history of music. Altogether too much of the educational solo music available almost exclusively presents work by minor or unknown composers.

The recordings we have made should be used only as a guide for you to use in studying a piece. We certainly didn't go into these recording sessions with the idea of trying to create any kind of "definitive performances" of this music. There is no such thing as a definitive performance anyway. Each musician, being a unique individual, will naturally always come up with a slightly different rendition of a piece of music. We often find that students are timid about revealing their own ideas and personalities when going beyond the notes on the page in making music. After you've practiced for weeks or months on a piece of music, and have mastered all the technical requirements, you certainly have earned the right to play it in the way you think it sounds best! It may not be the way your friend would play it, or the way The Canadian Brass would play it. But you will have made the music your own, and that's what counts.

Good luck and Happy Brass Playing!
The Canadian Brass

FRED MILLS had an extensive performing career that preceded his joing the Canadian Brass. He grew up in Guelph, Ontario. After graduating from the Juilliard School of Music, he became principal trumpet under conductor Leopold Stokowski in both the American and Houston Symphonies. He also performed under Pablo Casals at the Casals Festival, and has play´d at the Marlboro Music Festival. For six years Fred was principal trumpet of the New York City Opera orchestra. Following this, he returned to Canada to take a position as principal trumpet of the then newly formed National Arts Centre Orchestra in Ottawa. Fred left this orchestra to join The Canadian Brass in the quintet's formative stages.

RON ROMM was a child prodigy as a trumpet player, beginning his career as a soloist at the age of ten. By twelve, he was a member of his family's band, age eighteen he was performing regularly with the Los Angeles Philharmonic. Ron attended the Juilliard School, and while in New York established himself as a top freelance trumpeter in the city, performing with everything from the New York Philharmonic to the Radio City Music Hall Symphony Orchestra to Broadway shows (like Sondheim's *Company*) to the circus tours and ice shows. Ron joined The Canadian Brass in 1971, just when the group had been together about a year. Although he has little time for performing outside the extensive Canadian Brass concert schedule, he is sought after as a pre-eminent soloist in many musical styles.

BILL CASEY, pianist, grew up in Atlanta, and holds degrees in piano from Louisiana State University and the University of Missouri at Kansas City. He was assistant editor on the new G. Schirmer Opera Anthology, and has recorded several other albums for Hal Leonard.

TRUMPET AIR

TRUMPET

George Phillipp Telemann

LYDIA

TRUMPET

Gabriel Fauré

RONDEAU

TRUMPET

Henry Purcell

ARIETTA
(Gia il sole dal Gange)

Alessandro Scarlatti

TRUMPET

GYPSY SONG
(Stride la vampa)
from
IL TROVATORE

TRUMPET

Giuseppe Verdi

DANCE A CACHUCHA
from
THE GONDOLIERS

Words by W.S. Gilbert
Music by Arthur Sullivan

TRUMPET

Tempo di Cachucha

TRUMPET

SERENADE
(Ständchen)

TRUMPET

Johannes Brahms

SOLACE

TRUMPET

Scott Joplin
Arr. by Rick Walters

Repeats are optional throughout.

TRUMPET

TRUMPET

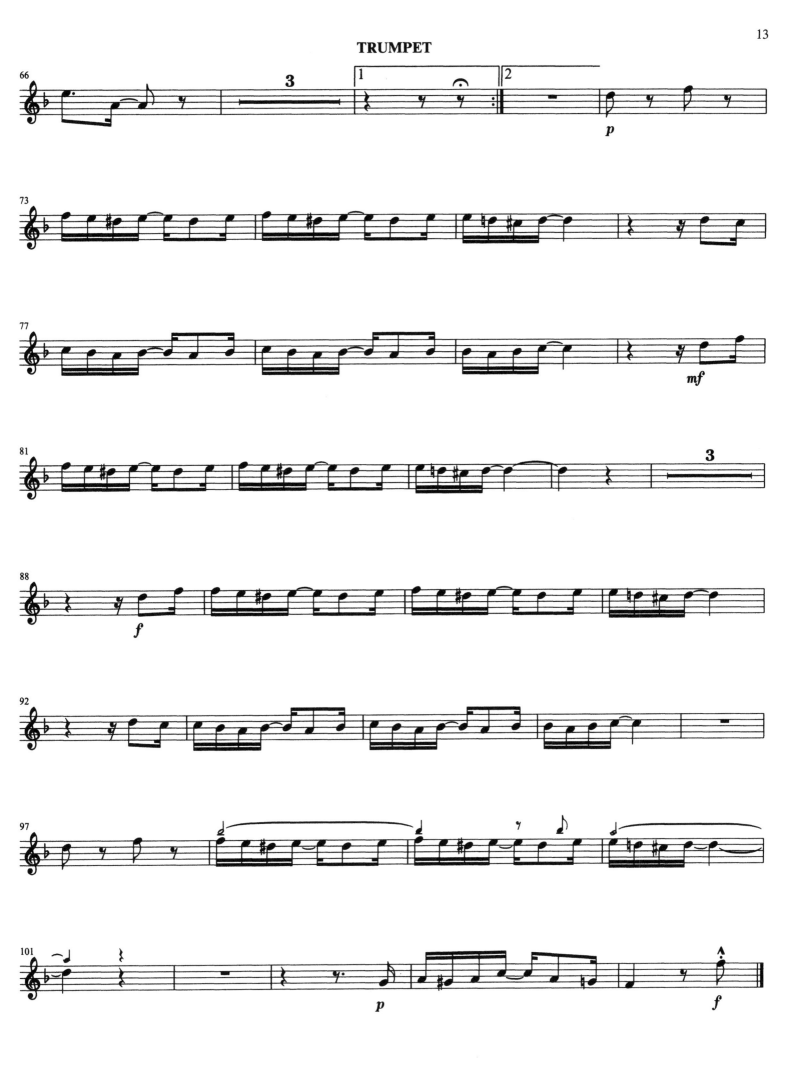

THE BROOK
(Wohin?)

Franz Schubert

TRUMPET

TRUMPET

MANDOLIN

TRUMPET

Claude Debussy

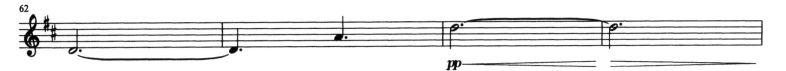

CLEOPATRA'S LAMENT

(Piangero, la sorte mia)

from

JULIUS CAESAR

TRUMPET

George Frideric Handel

TRUMPET

LA DANZA
(The Dance)
Neopolitan Tarantella

Gioachino Rossini

TRUMPET

TRUMPET